Photo Memories in Fabric

Album
Coverups

Lynda Milligan

&

Nancy Smith

POSSIBILITIES®

…Publishers of DreamSpinners® patterns,
I'll Teach Myself® sewing products, and Possibilities® books…

POSSIBILITIES®

…Publishers of DreamSpinners® patterns, I'll Teach Myself® sewing products, and Possibilities® books…

Credits

Sharon Holmes — Editing, Page Layout, & Production Art
Debbe Linn — Design, Cover, Photo Styling, & Production Art
Sara Tuttle — Design & Illustration
Sara Felton — Promotional Copy
Jane Dumler — Consulting & Inspiration
Brian Birlauf — Photography

Photo Memories in Fabric: Album Coverups
©1997 Lynda Milligan & Nancy Smith

ISBN: 1-880972-31-X

Introduction

Dear Friends,

In past books, we have shared photos of our family with you in photo transfer projects. When we saw the first memory books made by friends, we were happy to have discovered another creative way to showcase our prized photography. As our pages piled up, we began to group them into theme books. It is amazing to see the kids changing from year to year in the Halloween and Christmas books, to say nothing of our hairstyles and fashion sense!

As our shelves filled with scrapbooks, and we passed them around at family gatherings, we began to wonder if there were some way to individualize the book covers and protect them from wear and tear. That's how **this** book came to be. We decided to combine our love of fabric with our newfound scrapbooking obsession.

We hope you enjoy extending your creativity to the covers of your memory books. Don't forget that all of the motifs and drawings in this book can be enlarged or reduced to decorate your pages as well.

Happy scrapbooking!

Nancy & Lynda

Notebook Cover

Materials For One Cover

oversized 3-ring binder made especially for scrapbooks (approx. 11 1/2" tall by 12 1/2" wide*)

1/2 yd. 45" wide cotton fabric for cover (1 1/8 yds. if fabric is directional)

scrap fabrics for appliques (see color photos for inspiration)

approx. 1 yd. fusible web (such as Wonder-Under® Transfer Web)

1 1/8 yds. heavy or craft-weight iron-on interfacing thread

optional: spray fabric protector**

*Other binder sizes will work with the applique designs. See Notebook Specifics, page 5. The binders we like best are oversized to protect edges of pages, usually have D-rings, and fold back at spine.

We recommend spraying all fabrics **before using with a fabric protector such as Scotchgard™.

Directions

1. Lay interfacing adhesive side down on table. Lay open binder on interfacing, centering it from end to end and top to bottom.

2. Mark around binder on interfacing with a pen or pencil. Hold pencil upright while marking. Mark four short vertical lines to show position of spine. Remove binder.

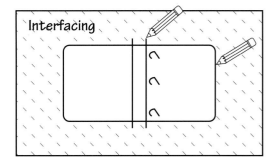

3. Connect the short vertical marks to complete the spine position markings. To mark cutting line, mark a line outside the binder line that is 1″ from each long side and 5″ from each short side. Cut out interfacing on the cutting line.

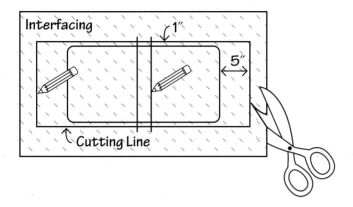

4. Cut a piece of cover fabric 2″ bigger in each direction than the interfacing. Lay fusible side of interfacing on wrong side of fabric cover, centered. Bond interfacing to fabric, following manufacturer's directions. Cut off excess fabric to match interfacing.

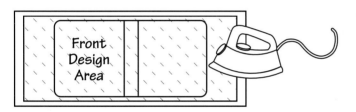

5. On all edges, fold 1/4″ to wrong side and stitch, forming a hem.

6. Transfer Front Edge Line to right side of cover by placing pins end to end on the right side. Transfer Front Spine Line to right side of cover in the same way. The space between the pin lines is the front design area.

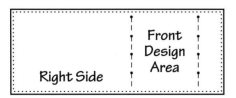

7. Fusible Applique: Place rough side of fusible web against desired pattern. **Patterns are printed in reverse for easy tracing to fusible web.** Trace shapes to paper side, leaving a little space between shapes.

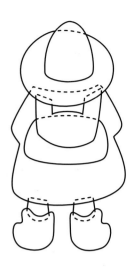

When pieces must overlap, add 1/8–3/16″ to the underneath piece. It helps to use a dotted line for this underlap when tracing.

Cut shapes apart. Do not cut on the lines. Place rough side of fusible web against **wrong** side of fabric. Bond according to manufacturer's directions. Cut out shapes on the lines and gently peel off backing paper.

Using pin lines and top and bottom edges of cover as guides, center pieces on front cover. Remember that 3/4″ at top and bottom will be lost in the facing. Remove pins. Bond design to cover following manufacturer's directions. Add eyes and detail lines with penstitch. Do not put spine label on at this time.

Note: To line white or very light fabrics, fuse to a layer of white fabric with fusible web, then fuse the traced pattern to the white lining.

Machine applique the edges of the pieces with a blanket stitch in colored thread, or use a small open zigzag and invisible thread. Buttonhole is tiny, about 1/8″ wide and 1/8″ apart. Each fabric shape as well as squares should be stitched down. See color photos for more detail.

Place squares & rectangles edge to edge

8. Fold front end of cover over, right sides together, along penciled Front Edge Line. Machine baste 1/8″ to 1/4″ outside top and bottom binder lines. (This depends on the thickness of your binder.) Turn right side out and try on binder so adjustments can be made. Cover should fit snugly. Adjust seams if necessary. Restitch with normal stitch length. Repeat basting for back edge of cover. (If your binder is particularly thick, the Back Edge Line may have to be moved out about 1/4″ as shown. When correct fit is established, restitch with normal stitch length. See diagrams in next column.

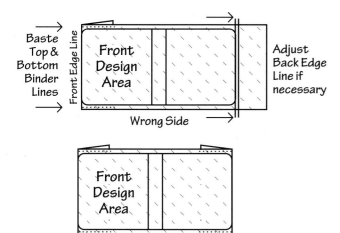

Baste Top & Bottom Binder Lines →

Front Edge Line

Front Design Area

Adjust Back Edge Line if necessary

Wrong Side

Front Design Area

9. Turn cover right side out. Finger press facing formed at top and bottom edges to the inside.

Front Design Area

10. Fuse Spine Label: Put cover on binder. Center spine letters and/or background rectangle on spine. Fuse to cover. Remove cover. Machine applique.

11. Open out binder and slide front and back edges of binder into cover.

Notebook Specifics

All of the cover designs can be adapted to fit binder covers that are not as wide as the ones we used. For example, on the Celebrations cover, leave off the lettering rectangle. Check the following paragraphs for adaptation suggestions for each notebook.

Celebrations — For narrower binder cover, leave off the lettering rectangle. See pages 10-11 for patterns.

Christmas — For narrower binder cover, leave off the lettering rectangle and Santa's bag. See pages 12-13 for patterns.

It's a Girl — For narrower binder cover, leave off the lettering rectangle and one of the ducklings. See pages 14-15 for patterns.

It's a Boy — For narrower binder cover, leave off the lettering rectangle and one of the train cars. See pages 15-16 for patterns.

School Days — For narrower binder cover, leave off the lettering rectangle and one of the apples. See pages 25-26 for patterns.

Halloween — For narrower binder cover, change the spacing between trick-or-treaters, or raise the center character up into the arch of the lettering. Three extra characters included are ghost, witch, and pirate. See pages 26-29 for patterns.

My Family — Head fabric will probably need to be lined. After cutting and fusing heads and hair, trace facial features on tracing paper with a pencil. Place traced designs, pencil side down, on faces. When face is in a pleasing position, trace again, and penciled lines will be lightly transferred to fabric. Use permanent markers to mark over the lines. Use a red pencil to add color to cheeks. For narrower binder cover, use six of the faces. See pages 30-31 for patterns.

Vacations — For narrower binder cover, leave off part of the left side of each of the four horizontal motifs and wrap part of lettering banner onto spine if necessary or leave off airplane and notch straight edge of banner. See pages 32-34 for patterns.

Wedding/Anniversary — For an anniversary, add the anniversary year in the center of the heart. Patterns page 35. Lettering page 38.

Winter — White fabrics will probably need to be lined. For narrower binder cover, leave off the tree. See pages 36-37 for patterns.

Lots of other ideas for using the patterns in this book!

Designs can be enlarged or reduced on a copier to fit your projects.

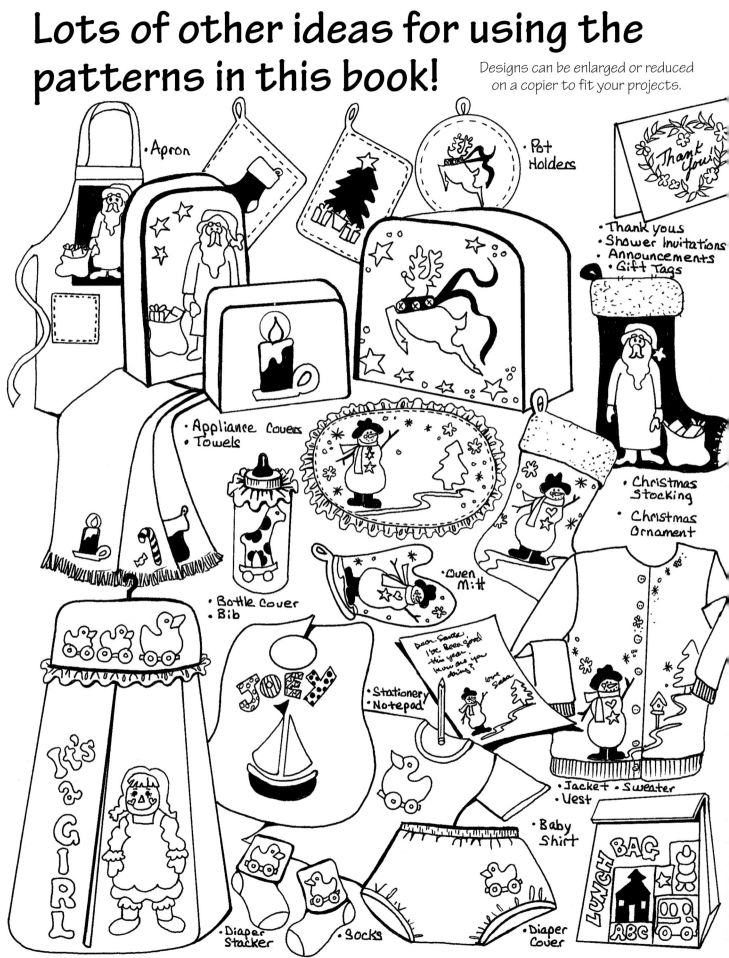

- Apron
- Pot Holders
- Thank yous
- Shower Invitations
- Announcements
- Gift Tags
- Appliance Covers
- Towels
- Christmas Stocking
- Christmas Ornament
- Bottle Cover
- Bib
- Oven Mitt
- Stationery
- Notepad
- Jacket • Sweater
- Vest
- Baby Shirt
- Diaper Stacker
- Socks
- Diaper Cover

• Ring Bearer's Pillow

• Gift Tag

To: From:

• Gift Bag

HALLOWEEN

• Wall Hanging • Banner • Quilt • Bulletin Board

• T-Shirt
• Gift Bag
• Invitation
• Card
• Gift Tag

• Placemat
• Apron
• Wall Hanging

Lunch Bag School Bag Tote

Grandma's Brag Book

• Grandma's Brag Book

• Eyeglass Case

From:

8

side your scrapbook!

Use the applique designs and the borders in this book to complement your scrapbook pages. The ideas on these two pages will jump-start your creativity. Also see some page ideas with the color photos. The puppy on the My Family page was colored in with markers. The border design from the Celebrations page comes from page two, and the balloons from the applique pattern. For the Christmas page we used applique patterns and the candy cane from this page.

CELEBRATIONS

Cut diploma
rectangle 1½x9"

Penstitch lettering & curled
paper lines at left end

Cut firecracker
rectangle 3x9"

CELEBRATIONS

Patterns are reversed
for easy tracing
to fusible web

Cut party hat
rectangle 3¼x5½"

Use same lettering & rectangle for spine

Cut cake rectangle
5½x5¾"

Cut lettering
rectangle 2x10"

Cut candy rectangle 2x4"

CHRISTMAS

Penstitch Santa's eyes & sleeve lines

Cut candle square 2x2"

Cut stocking
rectangle 2x3"

Cut Santa
rectangle 6x8",
then cut out 2x5"
from top left corner

Cut lettering rectangle 2x7"
Use same lettering & rectangle for spine

Penstitch reindeer's
eye & bell centers

Cut reindeer square 5x5"

Cut tree
rectangle 3x5"

CHRISTMAS

Patterns are reversed
for easy tracing
to fusible web

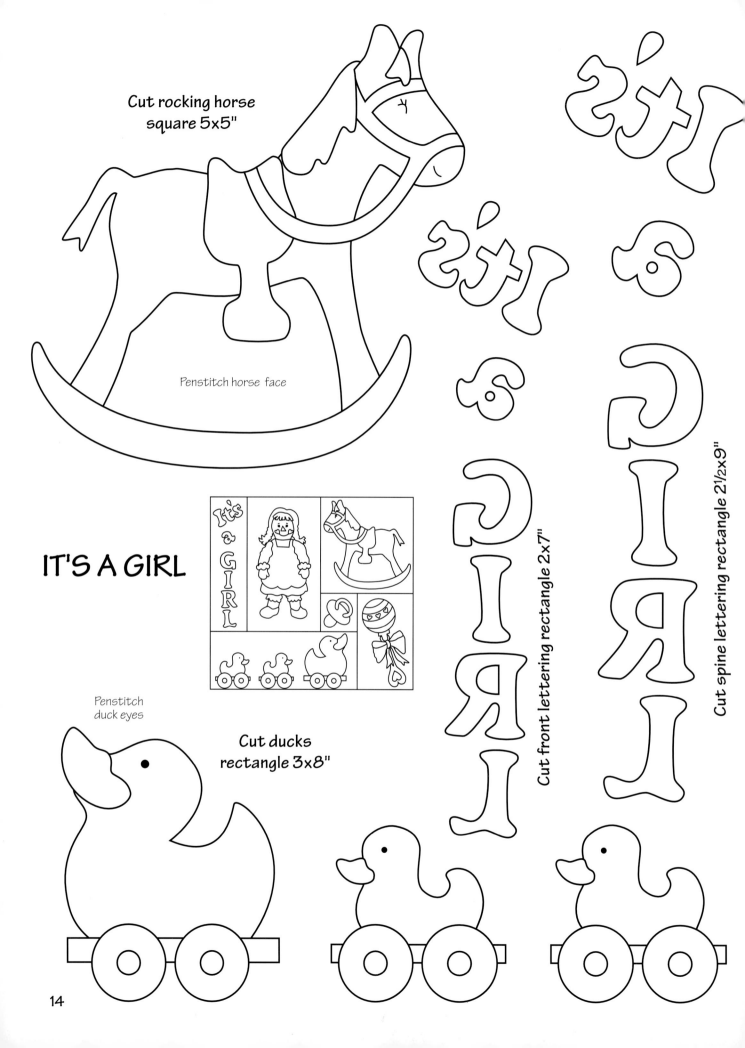

Cut rocking horse
square 5x5"

Penstitch horse face

IT'S A GIRL

Penstitch
duck eyes

Cut ducks
rectangle 3x8"

Cut front lettering rectangle 2x7"

Cut spine lettering rectangle 2½x9"

14

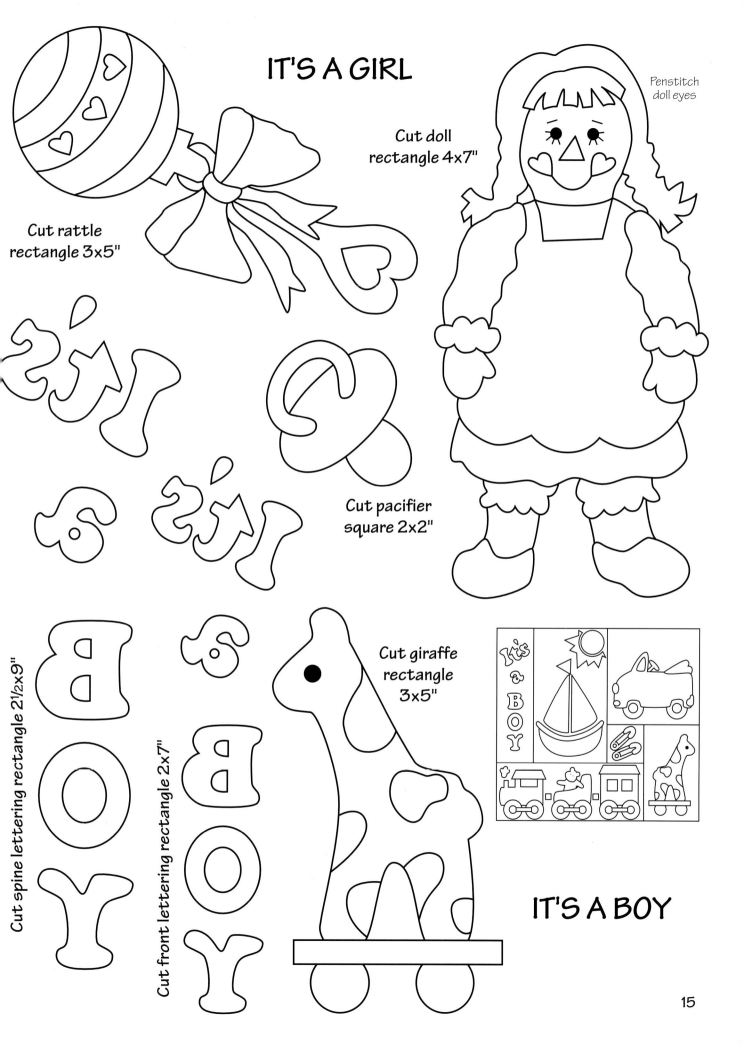

IT'S A GIRL

Penstitch doll eyes

Cut doll rectangle 4x7"

Cut rattle rectangle 3x5"

Cut pacifier square 2x2"

Cut spine lettering rectangle 2½x9"

Cut front lettering rectangle 2x7"

Cut giraffe rectangle 3x5"

IT'S A BOY

15

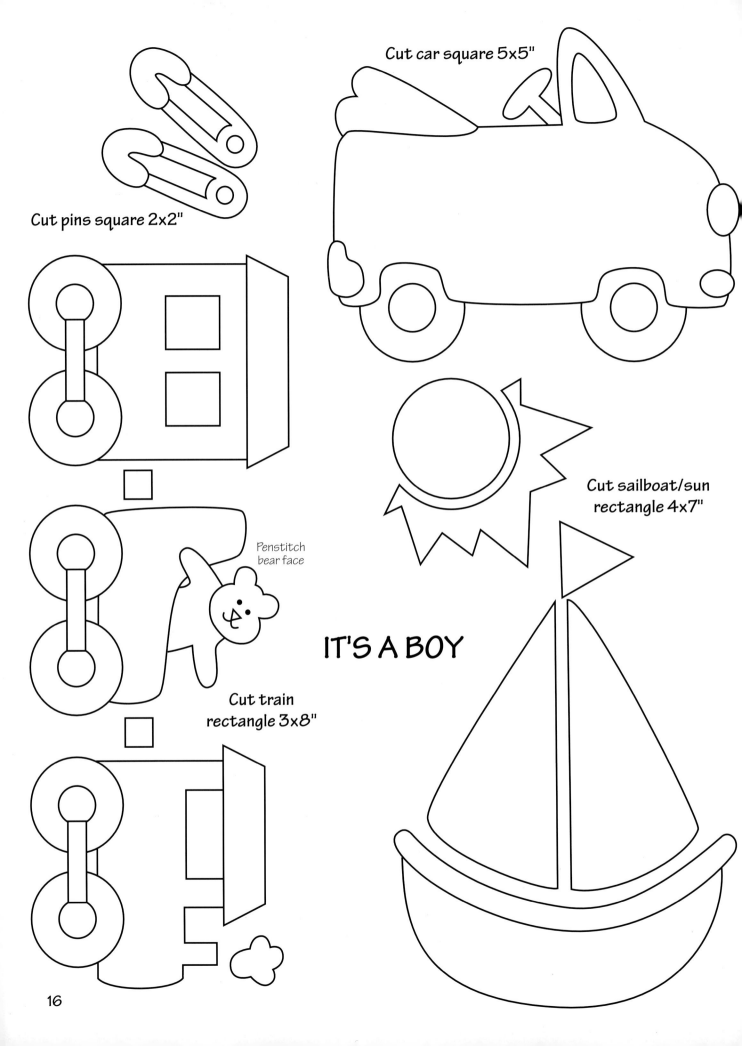

Cut car square 5x5"

Cut pins square 2x2"

Penstitch bear face

Cut sailboat/sun rectangle 4x7"

IT'S A BOY

Cut train rectangle 3x8"

16

Make your own gift tags

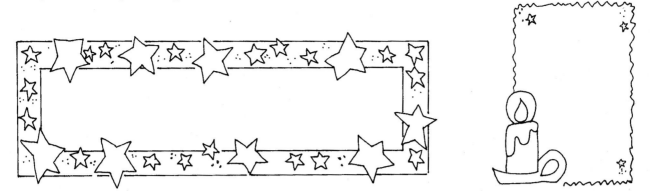

Come to the Halloween party!

Where:_____

When:_____

Whooo:_____

r.s.v.p. _____
or r.i.p.

And Bring Your Pal!

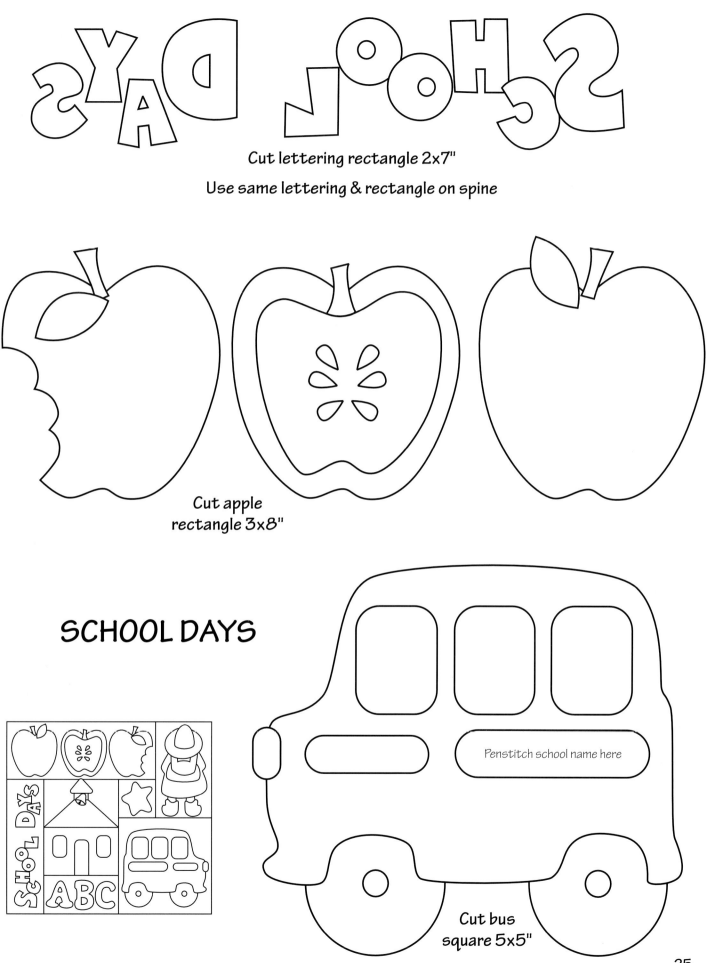

Cut lettering rectangle 2x7"

Use same lettering & rectangle on spine

Cut apple
rectangle 3x8"

SCHOOL DAYS

Penstitch school name here

Cut bus
square 5x5"

Cut ABC rectangle 2x4"

SCHOOL DAYS

Penstitch bell clapper

Cut schoolhouse rectangle 4x5"

Cut star square 2x2"

HALLOWEEN

Cut girl rectangle 3x5"

Not pictured

HALLOWEEN

Patterns are reversed
for easy tracing
to fusible web

Tail wraps onto spine

HALLOWEEN

Front

Not pictured

Penstitch
lines on patch &
detail lines on feet

Back

Not pictured

HALLOWEEN

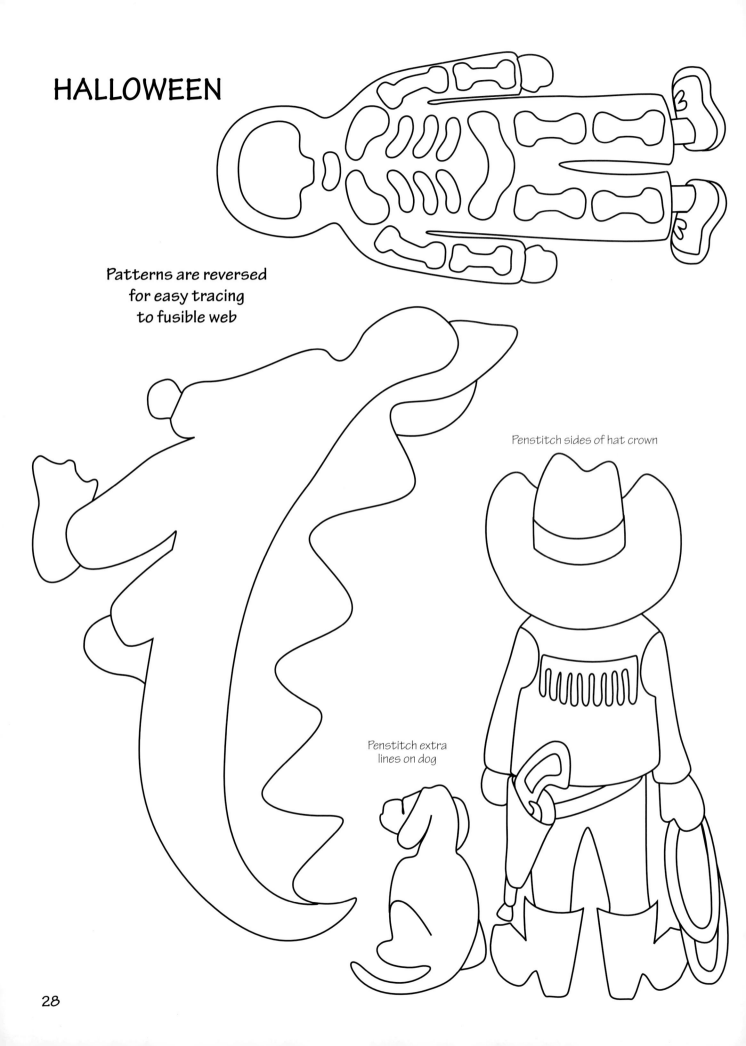

Patterns are reversed
for easy tracing
to fusible web

Penstitch sides of hat crown

Penstitch extra
lines on dog

28

Try gold rick rack for the antennae

Grandpa

Cut background rectangles 3½x3"
& place them ³/8" apart on cover

Teen Boy

Dad

Grandma

Young Boy

Penstitch
facial features

Pet Cat

Teen
Boy

Grandma

Dog
Topknot

Pet Dog

MY FAMILY

Trace face shapes on tracing paper & then design your own
family members by mixing hairstyles, clothing, & facial features

Cut background rectangles 3½x3" & place them 3/8" apart on cover

MY FAMILY

Grandpa

Young Girl

Baby

For boy baby, leave off bow & cut scallops off bib

Baby

Mom

Use this lettering for spine. Use fabric scraps from background rectangles for letters.

Baby Bonnet

Young Girl

Mom

Face fabric may need to be lined

Teen Girl

31

VACATIONS

Penstitch banner rope

Use same lettering on a 2½x9" rectangle for spine

Cut sailboat sky rectangle 2¼x11"

Match dotted line when tracing mountains, ground, & lake

Cut cabin sky rectangle 2½x11"

Penstitch fish eye

Match dotted line when tracing mountains, ground, & lake

Patterns are reversed
for easy tracing to fusible web

Cut desert sky rectangle 2½x6"

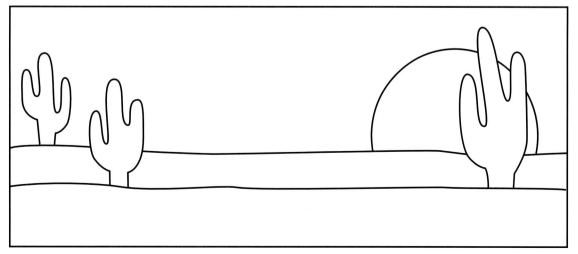

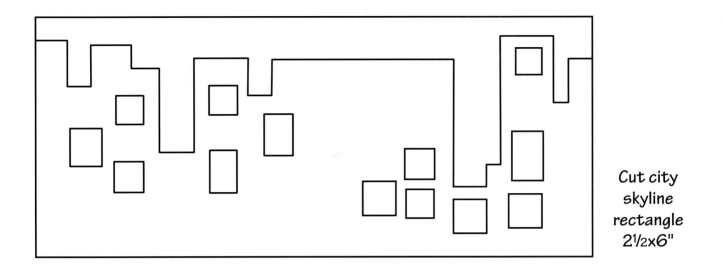

Cut city
skyline
rectangle
2½x6"

Penstitch skier's face

Cut skier's green
forest square 5x5"

White snow fabric
may need to be lined

Use alphabet on page 38 for lettering.
Add a small flower at top & bottom
of lettering on spine ("WEDDING").

For anniversary albums, applique
years (50th) in center of heart

WEDDING/ANNIVERSARY

WINTER

Penstitch
mouth

Front

Back

36

Use this lettering on spine
with no background rectangle

WINTER

Penstitch
mouths

Penstitch
dog's eyes

37

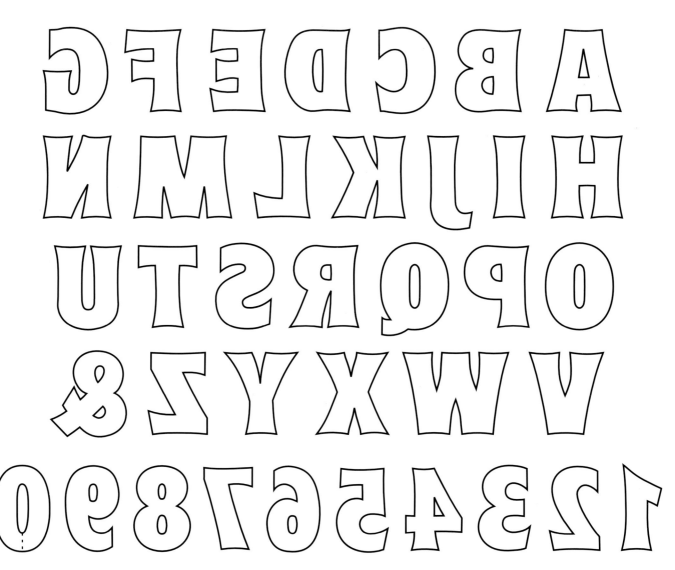

To cut circles in letters, slit fabric (see dotted line on O)

MORE CREATIVE WAYS TO ACCENT YOUR SCRAPBOOKS!

Applique motifs can easily be adapted to decorate pages of memory books. Whether you are ready to put pictures to paper or needle to fabric, you are sure to find more inspiration in these quality books from Possibilities®.

Snow Gear

Snowmen, ski trips, ice-skating, and sledding. Outdoor excursions in the cold winter months can warm your heart for years to come when you create a memory book with your pictures and our motifs from Snow Gear. Fused appliques and buttonhole stitching make this a great first-time project or quick project for more experienced quilters.

Simply Fuse & Use

Adding the color and texture of fabric to our lives is easy with the step-by-step technique explained in Simply Fuse & Use. Album covers are just the beginning when sharing your love of fabric and making your scrap bag work for you. Ideas given for creative use of fabric, preprinted panels, and border prints. More than 50 easy and quick projects. Great gift ideas!

Pillow Patches and Calendar Patches

These books contain more than 50 simple fused applique designs. Ideas for every month of the year leap off the pages of our books onto your memory pages. Making pillows has never been so easy or so much fun. Pillow covers can be changed at the flip of a button.

Here Comes Santa Claus

Doesn't everyone have a shoebox full of happy holiday pictures that they would like to share in a memory book? Decorate your book with the north woods flavor of the Here Comes Santa Claus motifs. Step-by-step directions make it easy for anyone from beginner to expert to make projects including a quilted banner, pillow, sweatshirt, vest or even stationery.

Penstitch & Lettering

Penstitch & Lettering is the perfect reference for scrapbooking! It contains five alphabets and a wealth of line art, drawings, and sayings for you to trace and copy into memory books. Personalize almost anything in minutes—more than 150 delightful designs.

P.S. I Love You and P.S. I Love You Two!

Are you making a memory book for new baby? Applique motifs, as well as the charming illustrations throughout these books, make cute and cuddly complements to your little one's pictures. Each book contains 17 quilts in cradle, crib, and twin sizes, as well as complete directions and a multitude of techniques.

✳ ✳ Coming soon: **More Penstitch & Lettering** ✳ ✳

Don't forget the other book in our
Photo Memories in Fabric series!

Quilts & More

This colorful collection of future heirlooms includes easy-to-sew projects using photo transfers. Quilts, pillows, and wall hangings display treasured photographs that capture the memories of our lives.

PHOTO TRANSFERS RESOURCE

If you can't find photo transfer paper or need someone to make transfers, please send a SASE for our brochure.

POSSIBILITIES®

8970 E. Hampden Ave. • Denver, CO 80231
Orders Only U.S. & Canada 1-800-474-2665
Phone 303-740-6206 • Fax 303-220-7424